MAPLE SYRUP

HARVEST TO HOME

Lynn M. Stone

Rourke Publishing LLC
Vero Beach, Florida 32964

www.rourkepublishing.com

PHOTO CREDITS:
All photos © Lynn M. Stone

EDITORIAL SERVICES:
Pamela Schroeder

Library of Congress Cataloging-in-Publication Data

Stone, Lynn M.
    Maple syrup / Lynn M. Stone.
        p. cm. — (Harvest to home)
    Includes index.
    Summary: Describes the nature and making of maple syrup.
    ISBN 1-58952-128-5
    1. Maple syrup—Juvenile literature. [1. Maple syrup.] I. Title

TP395 .S76 2001
641.2'364—dc21   2001031664

Printed in the USA

TABLE OF CONTENTS

Maple Syrup   5

Maple Sap   11

Gathering   16

Boiling   22

Glossary   23

Index   24

Further Reading/Websites to Visit   24

MAPLE SYRUP

The sugar maple is a favorite North American tree. It offers people one gift after another.

The sugar maple has strong, hard wood for building. It has wide leaves for summer shade. Each fall it offers beauty with bright red, yellow, and orange leaves. The sugar maple also offers something tasty—maple syrup!

Sugar maples with their autumn leaves surround an old sugarhouse.

Maple syrup is a sweet, sticky liquid. It tastes and looks rich and yummy. Maple syrup is a beautiful golden yellow color called **amber**.

People pour maple syrup onto waffles and pancakes. They also use it to sweeten coffee, cereal, and ice cream. Maple syrup can be made into other **products**, like maple sugar, maple cream, maple butter, and maple candy.

Bottles of maple syrup line the shelves of a roadside stand in Vermont.

Most breakfast syrups in food stores are made from corn products. Corn syrup is much cheaper to make than maple syrup. Some corn syrup makers add maple syrup to make their product taste better.

Sugar maples are most common in the Northeast. Most maple syrup is made there. Vermont is the leading maple syrup maker in the United States. New York is second, followed by Wisconsin and New Hampshire. Quebec, in Canada, makes more maple syrup than all the United States together!

Sap collectors take a break and give the horses a drink of sweet maple sap.

MAPLE SAP

Maple syrup is made from sugar **maple sap**. Maple sap is a clear, watery liquid inside the trees.

In late winter and early spring, northern nights are cold. But days can be warm. Maple trees begin to "wake up" and sap begins to flow. This is the sugaring season. This is when sugar makers head to the woods, or the **sugarbush**.

Some sugar makers still gather sap the old-fashioned way, with a team of horses and a wooden dray on runners.

Most sugar makers collect maple sap in plastic pipelines.

Sweet smelling steam rises from boiling sap in a Vermont sugarhouse.

Sugar season lasts for about six weeks, starting in late February. But if it's very cold or very warm, that can change.

Sugar makers are people who make maple syrup. They are called sugar makers because maple syrup is full of natural sugars. In the past, maple sap was made into sugar far more often than syrup.

A sugar maker pipes new maple syrup into a barrel in the sugarhouse.

GATHERING

The first step in making maple syrup is to gather maple sap. People get maple sap in much the same way that the yellow-bellied sapsuckers do. The sapsucker is a woodpecker that loves tree sap. With its beak, the sapsucker drills little holes in a tree. The sap oozes through the holes. The sapsucker drinks the sap. Because the holes are small, the tree can heal itself easily.

A maple tree is quickly tapped with a drill.

Human sap collectors drill little holes, too. Each hole is less than 1/2 inch (almost 1 centimeter) wide and just 2 1/2 inches (6.5 centimeters) deep. This is called **tapping** the tree. Most trees have only one hole, or **tap**. Larger trees may have two, three, or four taps. The sap collector puts a small metal or plastic spout into the tap. Sap inside the tree flows into the tap and out the spout.

Maple sap drips through a metal spout. A pail will soon hang on the spout and collect sap.

The spout drips sap into a pail or into thin, soft, plastic pipeline. Sap flows downhill through the pipelines. Some sugar makers may have pumps that draw sap uphill a short way. The pipelines empty into tanks in the woods or the **sugarhouse**. The sugarhouse is the building where sap is made into maple syrup.

Sap that is collected in pails has to be emptied into a tank on a sleigh or truck. Then it is taken to the sugarhouse.

Sugaring crew empties sap pails into a tank on the dray.

BOILING

Maple sap tastes only a little sweet because it's mostly water. The sugar makers' job in the sugarhouse is to take out most of the water. To do that they boil the sap. Heat turns water into steam. The steam floats away, leaving behind pure, sugary maple syrup.

It takes about 40 gallons (151 liters) of sap to make 1 gallon (almost 4 liters) of syrup. It takes about four large, tapped sugar maples 6 weeks to make 40 gallons (151 liters) of sap.

GLOSSARY

amber (AM ber) — a deep yellow color

maple sap (MAY pel SAP) — the clear, watery liquid made by maple trees to carry the tree's food to its branches and leaves

product (PROD ekt) — that which is made or produced

sugarbush (SHOOG er boosh) — the woodland where sugar maple trees are tapped for sap

sugarhouse (SHOOG er hows) — the building in which maple sap is boiled to make syrup

tap (TAP) — the hole hammered into a sugar tree for the removal of sap

tapping (TAP ing) — the process of putting holes in sugar maple trees for the removal of sap

INDEX

maple sap   11, 14, 16, 19, 20, 22

New York   9

pipeline   20

Quebec   9

spout   19, 20

sugarbush   11

sugarhouse   20, 22

sugar makers   11, 14, 20, 22

sugar maple   5, 9, 22

tap   19

Vermont   9

Further Reading

Crook, Connie Brummel and Cameron, Scott (illustrator). *Maple Moon.* Stoddart Publishing, 1999.

Lynton, Marilyn and Fairfield, Lesley (illustrator). *The Maple Syrup Book.* Kids Can Press, 1993.

Websites To Visit

www.maple-erable.qc.ca (Quebec Maple Syrup Producers Federation)

www.uvm.edu (Proctor Maple Research Center)

About The Author

Lynn Stone is the author of more than 400 children's books. He is a talented natural history photographer as well. Lynn, a former teacher, travels worldwide to photograph wildlife in its natural habitat.